Kansas Whispers and Midnight Blues

Dodging Despair, Deception, and Clowns

Dale Goodvin

Back Seat Press

Back Seat Press
P.O. Box 974
Lakebay, WA 98349

ISBN: 978-0-6926256-0-6
LCCN: 2016901479
Published by Back Seat Press: Longbranch, WA, USA

Acknowledgements

Thank you to Ted Olinger for giving me such great and sensitive guidance in the writing of this book and who would not stop asking, "How's that book coming along, Dale?"

Thank you to Jerry Libstaff and his Watermark Writers group for insisting again and again that my poetry was moving and valuable to them.

Thank you, especially, to my wife, Trish, who lovingly supported me in my photographic and poetic struggles as I meandered my way through a number of twisted pathways in the process of creating this book.

Dedicated to my mother,
Nellie Grace Murray Goodvin
January 9, 1917 - September 9, 1949

and

To my aunt, Thelma Murray

Their love is always with me.

Kansas Whispers
and Midnight Blues

The geometry of innocence flesh on the bone
Causes Galileo's math book to get thrown
At Delilah who sits worthlessly alone
But the tears on her cheeks are from laughter

Bob Dylan

The whole future lies in uncertainty: live immediately.

Seneca

Contents

Kansas Whispers

Wrestling the Blues

Reflections of Restructured Realities

Love

Kansas Whispers

Outside/Inside

Everything is seen through
Mother and Father
In the darkness
Of lost eyes

Like lying down
On old yellow linoleum floors
Smelling of lonely days
And listening to the sound of panting dogs

Family Tree

I remember a tree in
My front yard
When I was six

It was a lovely tree
Tall and wide
With pink and white spring blossoms

Properly barren in winter
Bereft of spring beauty
Hung with winter's reminder that I had no mother

Echoes

Lunch is the noontime meal
And childhood still lingers

Eating alone in the school library
Six years old with ancient books

Echoes of a sandwich
Being unwrapped

And then dinner in a dusty room as twilight dims the world
Waiting silently for darkness to descend

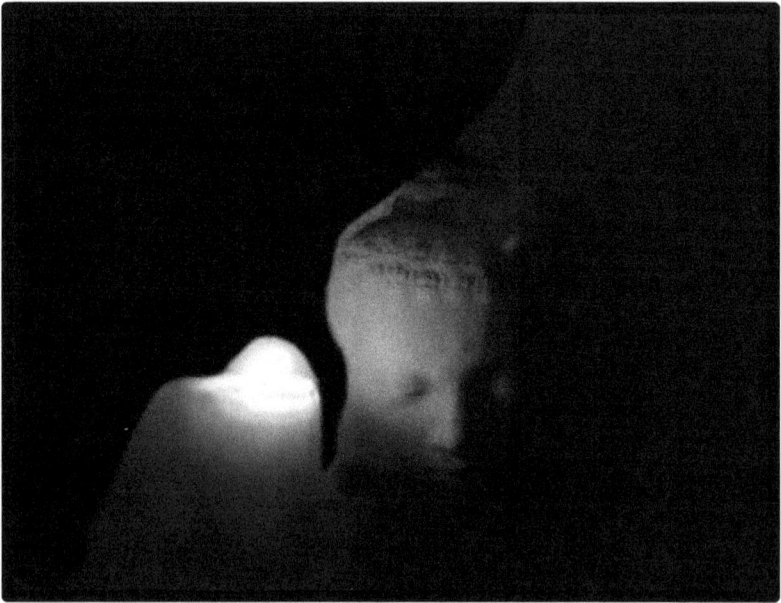

Mother/Father

Mother was a ghost
A wisp of light
Shadowy as night

A dead whisper
As I pulled up my covers
Against the cold

Father was an illusion
Bright outside
Dark within

Withholding love
For perfection
That never came

Walking the Road of an Unsweetened Destiny

He walked to school on a cold day
In his pajamas because he forgot
Where his t-shirt was
And he could not find his pants

And his mother was dead
And his father stank of anger
And he walked like a zombie
Relentlessly moving ever closer to school

Step by blind step by blind step
Wearing his pajamas on his thin body
Like a siren wailing during an early morning theft
Of a cheap car on a fucking used car lot

The Disguise Abides

What is lurking there in the shadows?
Who lingers on the edges?
Do growling dogs follow others too
Biting flesh as required by the laws
Of unbound fiends
Living in the minds
Of innocent lambs
Hiding in the backseat of dark blue 1953 Fords
Heading down the Kansas Highway at night
In a downpour of fog?

At Last

The smallest movement at the slightest beckoning
Can rock the ages
Can foul all senses and burn all reckoning
Can shred the souls of mighty sages

How death then must shake this world
So delicate is life to the smallest degree
That a mother's death unfurls for a child
As a ballet of frightful tragedy

Robins and Vultures

I woke up again with an uneasy mind
Negotiating, maneuvering
Listening to vultures

Pretending to be
Red robins
Bob bob bobbing in the air

Contemplating the repetitiveness
Of day and night
Wrapped in eternal embrace

Like quarreling lovers
Unable to recall
Lost affection

Back in the Day

Back in the day
Gasoline cost 25 cents a gallon
And coffee cost a nickel
And the wind howled across the flatlands of Kansas

And automobiles had hard metal dashboards
That could split your head wide open
And no seatbelts to hold you back
From a bloody windshield

And men wore hats to church
And women wore their best dresses
And little girls wore new shoes
And were filled with beauty and innocence

And boys were dressed in suits and ties
And the preacher scared us all
When he told us that hell was just a shot away
And that the gun had been fired

And that the bullet was headed our way
And that we better be very, very afraid
Back in the day the Kansas wind howled
And the dust blew and the trees sang the blues

Two Lanes

1953 Ford
Dark blue
Black highway
Two lanes

Rolling in Missouri
Hills
Curves
Two lanes

Farm tractor five miles an hour
Blistering sun
Windows down
Two lanes

No passing for miles
Heat shimmering
Dancing in the distance
Two Lanes

No passing
No passing
No passing
Two lanes

Dark

It was dark when I arrived
And found the pink rose on the driveway, lit brightly
By the glaring streetlight

It was dark when I arrived and heard the jazz the moment
I turned off the car, with the music filling the air with possibilities
Of a pink rose driving an old pickup down dusty roads

But I knew that the rose was of no significance
And did not represent love or romance
But was more like litter tossed by vagabonds

Creating hallucinations previously suppressed
Brought on by too much speculation
Into meanings and hopes and dreams

Of soft beds in motels with signs flashing
The night away in buzzing highway fluorescent
Symbols and metaphors

The world is crazy with pink roses
At night alone, promising truth
But poisoned with reality

Nibbling at the Edges

This shit is not always
In the middle of the goddamn stage
But it's always nibbling
At the edges

Waiting in the goddamn wings
Like a movie star
Counting his shiny gold coins and perfect
Sparkling diamonds

And I'm just a sad sap poor boy
Begging for a measly
Goddamn penny or two
In black and white desperation

Radio Days

When I was a young boy
My father and I
Listened to baseball games
On an old radio

In a hot dining room
On Kansas days
With a dingy green fan
Struggling to make life tolerable

Filling out our paper scorecards
With a number two pencil
That would tell the whole story
About every game

My father and I alone
Listening to the radio softly glowing pale orange
With a single light
Struggling against the darkness

Lent

I went to a real church as a boy in Kansas
And there was no need for an artificial Lent for us
Because girls could never wear pants or short skirts
Lent could hardly have made them purer

And there was never any blood-from-the-lamb-red
Fancy ass lipstick on women's lips turning them into
Cheap back alley harlots dressed in scarlet
How could Lent have purified them more

And those women in that church
I went to when I was a boy in Kansas
Never talked uppity-like to their men
Lent could not have shut them up any better

You see, we had already
Given up just about everything
No smoking or dancing or cussing
Or carousing and no music too

For us pure Protestants Lent was for a bunch of
Goddamn fish-eating Catholics
We had no use for any of it because we had our own
Moral compass pointing eternally to *no!*

That Kansas church hasn't moved an inch
Since I fled from it as though from the devil himself
Over sixty long years ago
Running like the wind

(Continued on next page)

So that I could dance a bit before
The past had a chance to catch up with me at last
So this Lent season I'm going to do
Some dancing and I'm going to do some singing

And I'm going to look at some
Long pretty legs in short skirts
While others give up stuff that I never ever had
When I was a boy in a church in Kansas

Saturday Morning

Refrigerator humming
Lights (some of them) on
Lights (some of them) off
Raining

Leaves on trees still as death
As broken watches
As yesterday
Hanging

Books beckoning
Words waiting
Failing
Falling

Like seeds
On a barren moon
In dark space
Dying

Morning Roses

I do not awaken
Happy like some,
Perhaps like soulful roses

I do not awaken
Into the light
But into gray shades

Pressing the covers
Down hard upon my conceptualizations
And upon time and space

I do not fight the moment
So that it will not fight me,
Before arising I wait for it

To soften to permutations
Of acceptable tolerances,
Perhaps like soulful roses

Wrestling the Blues

My Father's Son

I saw my father's son
In the mirror this morning
Same round face
He looked a lot like me

I saw my father's son
Hiding in the pale morning light
Cowering in the corner
Dreaming of the night

Where the shadows hide my father
Cruel to the bone and ready for a fight
As he whispers in my ear
In the ghostly moonlight

I saw my father's son in the mirror
And closed my eyes
And repeated my holy mantra
Be kind, be kind

Be kind to wretched memories
Be kind to frightened children
Be kind to a father's son
Who is hiding in the mirror

Riding Shotgun

As a boy I wanted to ride shotgun
In my father's car
In the front seat
Of an old black Ford

I should have started hitchhiking
To distant destinations
In the front seats
Of strangers' cars

I should have taken my shotgun and made my escape
Riding in a bright red Chevrolet
Hair swept back against the wind
On the road to Santa Fe

New Mexico Blues in Black and White

I feel like I am covered by a cheap black plastic tarp
In a goddamn stolen car hidden
In a stinking rat-infested garage
In a back alley in Albuquerque

Painted by a crazy drunk artist
Riding low on some copped heroin
And rented brushes and borrowed paint
In a back alley in Albuquerque

And the painting is cool
And the goddamn robins are singing
Like goddamn Frank Sinatra
And I am so fucking sad in a back alley in Albuquerque

Dancing on the Edges

No more dancing lightly
Like a ballet boy
On the edges of stages
With props of lies

No more playing tiddlywinks
To pass the day in twilights
Of make-believe victories
With pretend wars conquered

No more hiding in a hot Kansas alley
With tin cans littering the crumbled ground
With a clown asking me to sit on his knee
Telling me that his love was not for him but for me

The delicate deception dance is over
The violins have been burned, the stage is deserted
The lights have dimmed to a haunted glow
The play is over, the theater is closed

Solace

Destruction is gaining ground
Second by second
Along the avenue

Sharp winds in the alley corners
Fight with last second maneuvers
To ever fading imaginary draws

Negativity the only solace
But too heavy
To balance the load

I don't need no money
I don't need no dope
I need a change of heart

Preparing for the Rising Tide

Escaping the here and the now
Exhausts the days and nights
Blotting out even form and function

For the here and the now
Are so demanding of one's time
Of one's attention

That escaping them must be done righteously
In an unrighteous world
If the howling ghosts are to be disarmed

The Falling Snow

It started as a gradual descent
Not attaining steeper inclines
Until gradual was just another game of dice

Then the slope declined
To straight down
To what surely was meant to be the bottom

But the crash never came
Even though the speed seemed to attain supernatural levels
And I had no helmet anyway

So I just closed my eyes
In the downtown journey
To this bench in this city on this frozen day in the falling snow

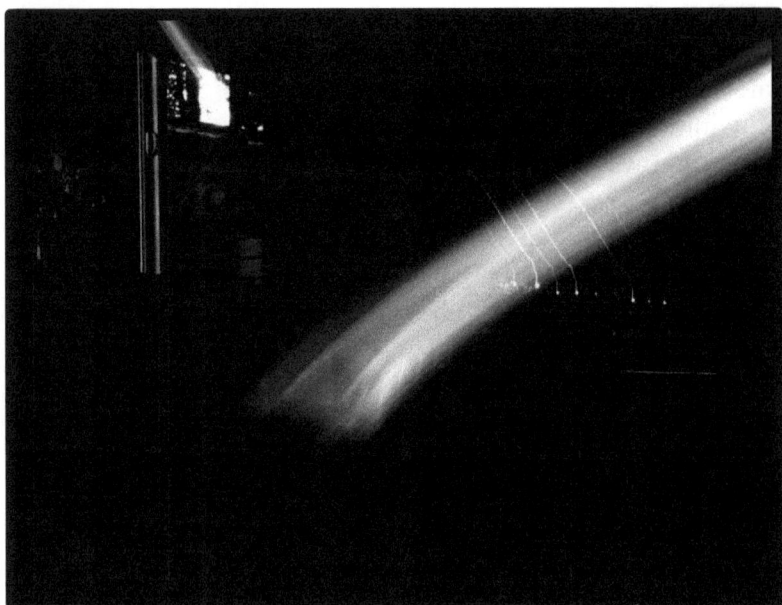

My Black Dog

Days and days and nights and nights trying
To remember what I forgot
After being ripped
Into existence

The voices
The words
The chilling cacophony
Of dissonance

The air freezing
Lights blazing
Colors exploding
No hiding

Solitude like
The morning sun rising
Shattered with the crowing
Of a million angry roosters

A black dog growls
The sun is eclipsed, the rain falls
A child weeps and forgets everything
But a black dog growling

Televisions on the Run in a World Gone Wrong on a Day Gone Bad

The roses were painted by a master
As was the hanging
As was the bumper crop of potatoes
As was the low-down shooting of the tinhorn sheriff

I was so scared of hanging
Last night in Albuquerque
That I forgot eternal truths
Like "don't look in no mirrors for the truth"

But none of it matters
Because goddamn it, color television
Is just black and white
Juiced up for losers

Perplexities

I am watching the sun set
In the sky
With clouds painting the day black

As the wind blows tree branches
Sending them to dance
With unsteady souls

The seconds surrendering
The minutes collapsing
The hours falling like slow motion punch-drunk boxers

And time wavers
And the present trembles
And my past never passes

And ghosts with red wings
Fly around me beckoning me home
Singing like a chorus of drowning swans in the falling rain

Shapes and Shadows

We are shapes and shadows drifting high and low
Down the alleys of broken glass shining
And glowing in slanted light bearing sharp images
Dragged from unconsciousness to cognitive
Dissonance to barely recognizable cornerstones
Of foundations built on elusiveness and shifting sands

And sinking and rising and drifting like smoke in a
Cheap diner where the meals are served
One by one by one by one by clowns in servers'
Outfits created by midnight dreamers
Dealing from the bottom of the deck and
Dancing the midnight rumba

We are shapes and shadows dreaming of solidity
Riding the black and white horses of dreams
Created in factories of delusions and illusions and
Confusions and conclusions drawn by fat lines on
Plates of tin falling to brittle floors from
Sailing trees in the night wind

And the blackened steep night
And the sunshiny and bright and dazzling
And blinding light
Flow on and on and on
In this haunted land
Of make believe

Reality

The real world is dead
It is over
Gone forever

Now concepts conquer,
Illusion collides with illusion
For the creation of data

That provides pale images and pretty graphs
Of life as portrayed on television
And no one knows

If the shows are what they seem
Or if they're downtown dreams
Hiding screams and schemes

The smiles seemed so real
As they were instructed to kneel on bended knees
Before the firing squads

Ripped them apart as the audience squealed
With childish delight
And it all seemed so … right

Bring 'em On

Bring on the dreams
Let them fill my eyes
With stardust
And tin rust

Let them break the watches
And fuck up the phones
And leave me alone
In a hidden zone

For dreams are easy
It is waking life
With mad frenzy
That stabs my heart with sharpened knives

Sad to the Bone

I got nothin' at home
I got nowhere to roam
I'm sad to the bone

I got got got the downtown blues
To the bottom of my shoes
I got nothin' to lose

I'm heading down on a one-way train
In the cold, cold rain
With a head full of pain

I got no one to phone
I'm dead-bound alone
I'm sad to the bone

Martyrs in the Mist

I am driving on a black highway
With tall green trees on both sides

Like martyrs in the mist
Like holy ghosts

With their souls
Swaying in the wind

Brothers and sisters
Mothers and fathers

I am driving on a black highway
Making my getaway from Kansas

Settling the Bet

For a dime, the clown smiled
For a quarter, he chuckled
For a dollar, he laughed outright

Such were the mechanisms of my life
In the circus of days
Called my childhood

The clown's smile was always an upside down frown
And the clown's chuckle was always a hidden gasp
And the clown's laughter never rang true

But I had to survive and smiles were like bandits
And chuckles were like midnight rodeos with broken horses
And laughing was an escape down a cold fire escape
In the dark of night

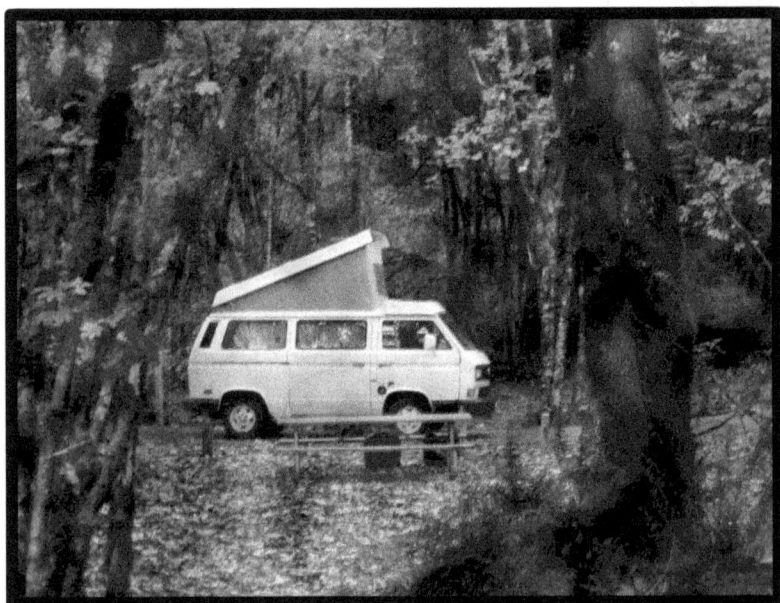

The Wrong Side of Town

I'm gonna remember that sad face
On the wrong side of town
Where the beat up bum
Was just another rundown clown

Gonna remember the slamming of doors
And the weeping of whores
And the grinding of gears
Stuck in shattered mirrors

Where babies are sold for a buck and a half
And mothers are put on the town square rack
For having long flowing hair that sails in the wind
For having love in their hearts to the very end

Gonna write a love poem about the hate in this world
Gonna write a love poem about the hate in this world
Gonna re-name the goddess they called a bitch
Gonna pull that sweetheart right outta the ditch

Gonna raise me an army
Recruit some bums and some hard-headed women
Gonna sharpen our blades on a cold afternoon
Gonna slay some dragons under a blood-red moon

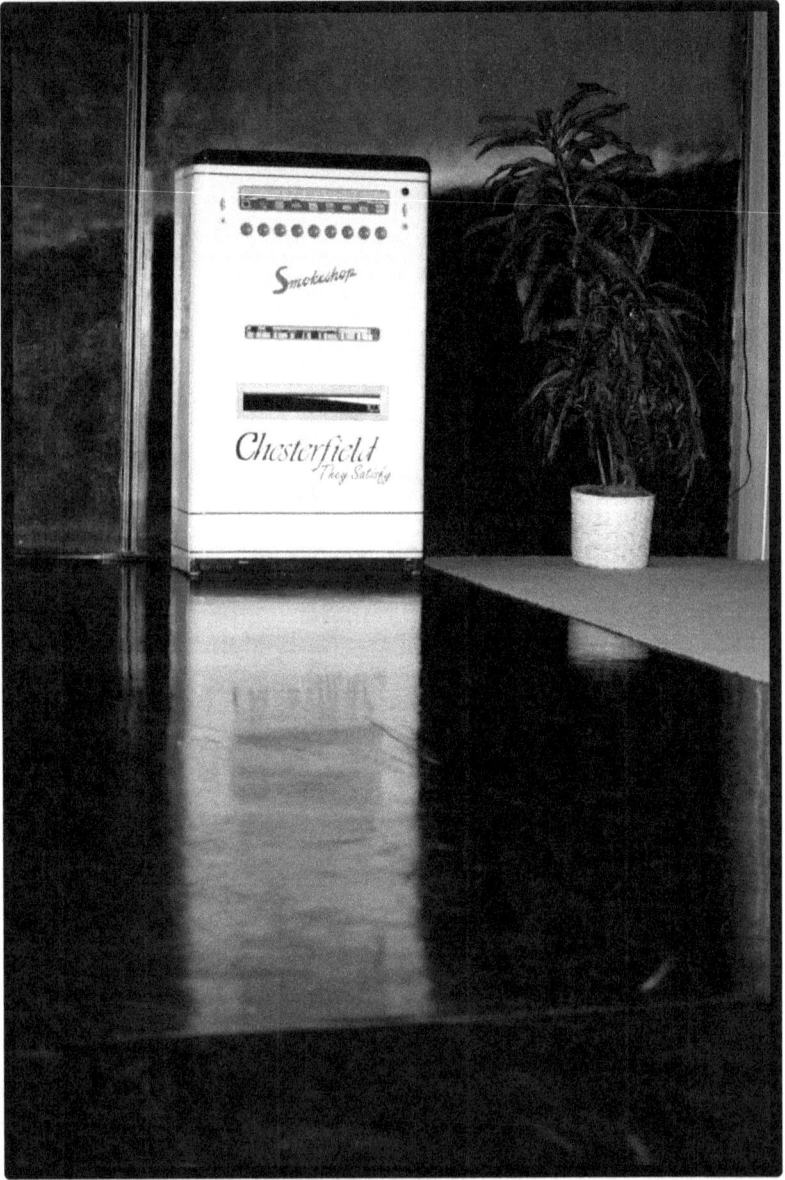

Oh Shit

Goddamn you
He said
To himself

You drunk shit
Here on the skids
Looking for cigarette butts

Goddamn you

We the People

"We the People" in Old Testament times were
A "stiff-necked" people
Who refused to yield either to Raining Frogs
Or Massive Boils on their desert dried skin

"Fuck you God, you ole miserable Bastard"
They wailed even as they trembled in fear
And bowed in supplication, hoping against hope
That the Son of a Bitch would yield before they slit
Their fucking throats to end it all

I have stood stiff-necked against
The same frogs, the same boils
I stand firm with my Old Testament
Brothers and sisters, claiming with them

That we will not take that shit no more
We will not take that shit no more
We shall overcome, you Sly Motherfuckers,
We shall overcome

At the Theater with LSD

Sweet Jesus we were high
As the movie arose from the unknown
And the light darkened
And the voices spoke

We lost Charlie
And found him wandering
The streets hours later
Looking for the theater

He had a big smile on his face
And said something like "Hi, ya"
And we all hugged and laughed
Like we always did back then when we were happy

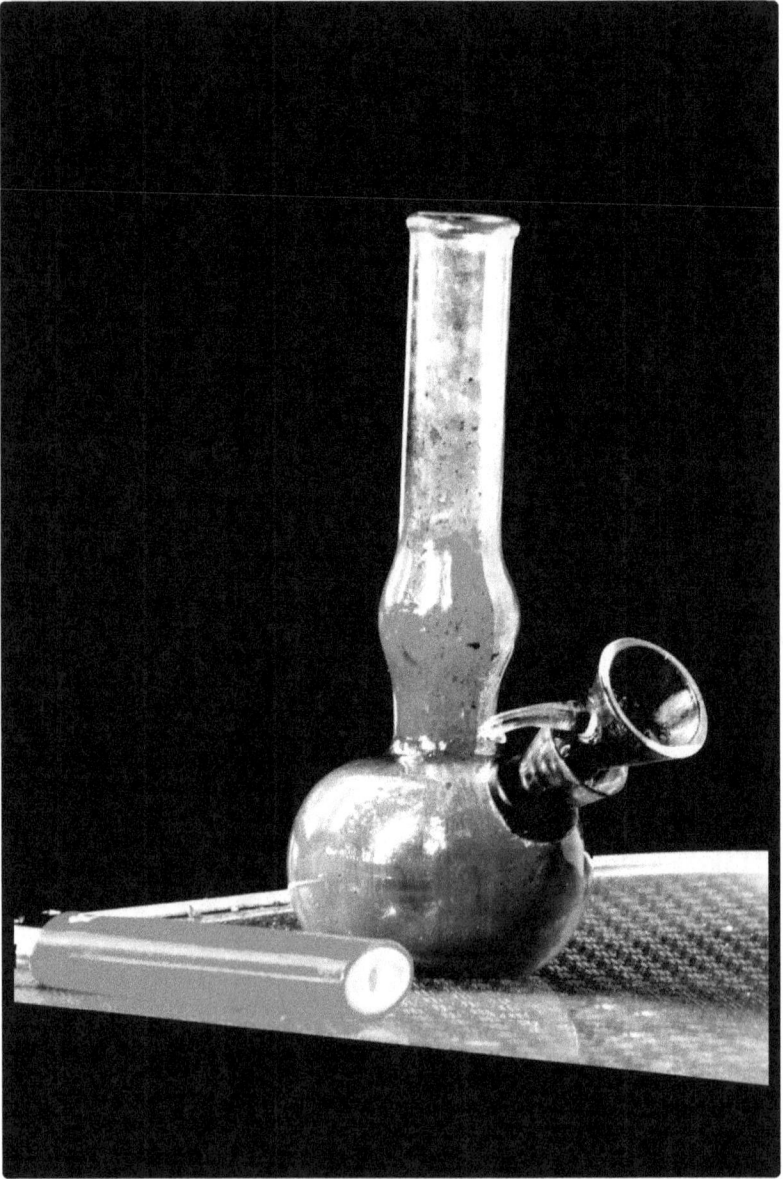

Peace and Love

I wore a peace symbol to beer joints
When war was raging in Vietnam
To make a drunken point
About America's bloody scam

I thought that peace and love
Painted on a brilliant poster
Fit me like a glove
Challenging death's roller coaster

Now I'm buried in the midnight snow while winds
Howl in the dark and dreams that were once glowing
Like stars in the sky have been smashed out
Of the fucking unholy ballpark

Orange, the Misunderstood Truth

Color fools the mind
Into believing that eyes
Can see and that
Orange can be defined, caged

Blink away the day
And the night
And the world
And embrace what is left

Step lively while you can dance
While you can glitter
While you glow
Step lively

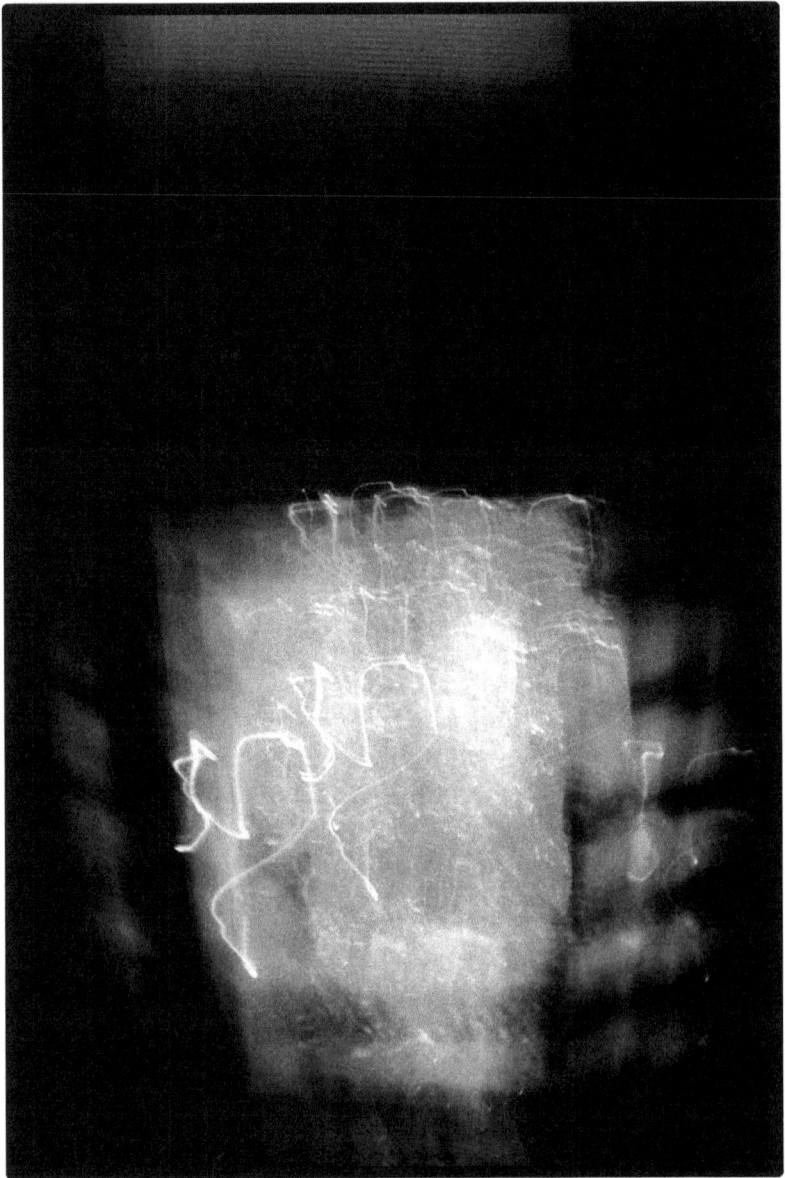

A Turn of the World

A turn of the world happens on a cheap dime
In a cheap alleyway of nighttime goons and daytime puppets

It happens as you blink something out of your eye
And you see truth's enemy grinning

It happens when the dogs bark at night
And you think the vampires have risen

It happens in the second when you drop your guard
And the buzzards start pecking

It happens as the crunch of dreams start crashing
And the lamb slays the lion and the boy eats the wolf

A turn of the world blasts in the heart
And you never see the bullet coming

The Foundation

Hang on to the foundation of the Cross, they say
Yet even Jesus Christ built fences topped
With barbed wire against the blood red sky above the
Pearly gates surrounded by shotgun guards and
Downtown pitchfork angels

Hang on to the foundation of the Truth, they say
Yet the truth may be no more than a cheap alibi
Told by a ruthless clown in a filth-strewn alley

Hang on to the foundation of your Heart, they say
Yet your heart may deceive you like the midnight
Rider leaping over a ghost land of broken promises in
A made-for-TV docudrama swallowed whole by
Hollywood dust in the broken light of a high-noon gunfight

Hang on to the foundation of the Warrior, they say
Yet those who demand final conquest when
The frozen winter moon begins to bleed turn out to be
Monster werewolves weeping like babies

And the Holy Saint and the Homeless Bum await the
Same salvation praying that the Final Kiss of Death
And Embrace of Eternity will save them at last when
They roll their wretched dice and float into Emptiness

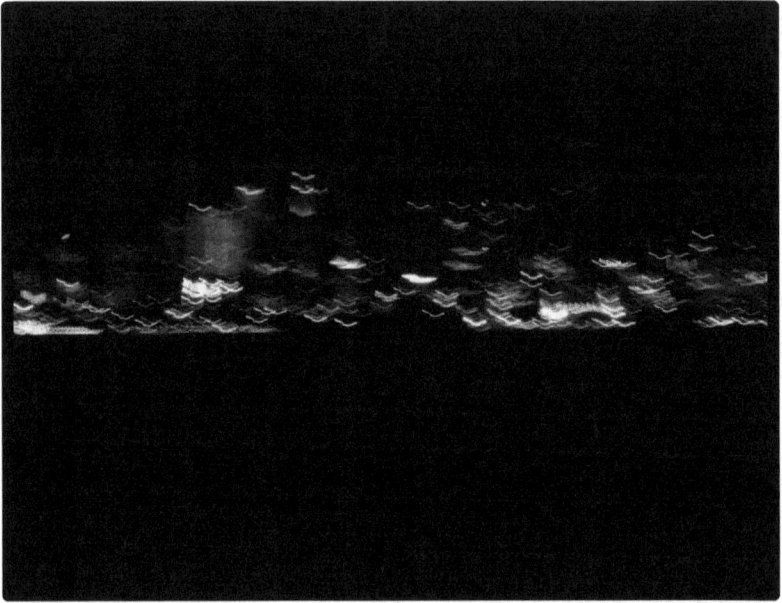

Morning Thoughts

Rise from sleep as an angel
Flying over the enemy
Carrying bombs to drop
On children and old people
On dogs and cats

Rise from sleep as the truth weeps
In the futility
Of trying to ward off
The flapping noise of vampire wings
In a room of ghosts

Father ghosts with belts that swing
And dead Mother ghosts with hearing aids that don't work
And hungry ghosts
And lonely ghosts
And shivering ghosts

Every morning: rise rise rise!
Re-memorize the alphabet!
Re-memorize multiplying and adding and subtracting!
Re-memorize your own name!
Battle your past in its fierce grave!

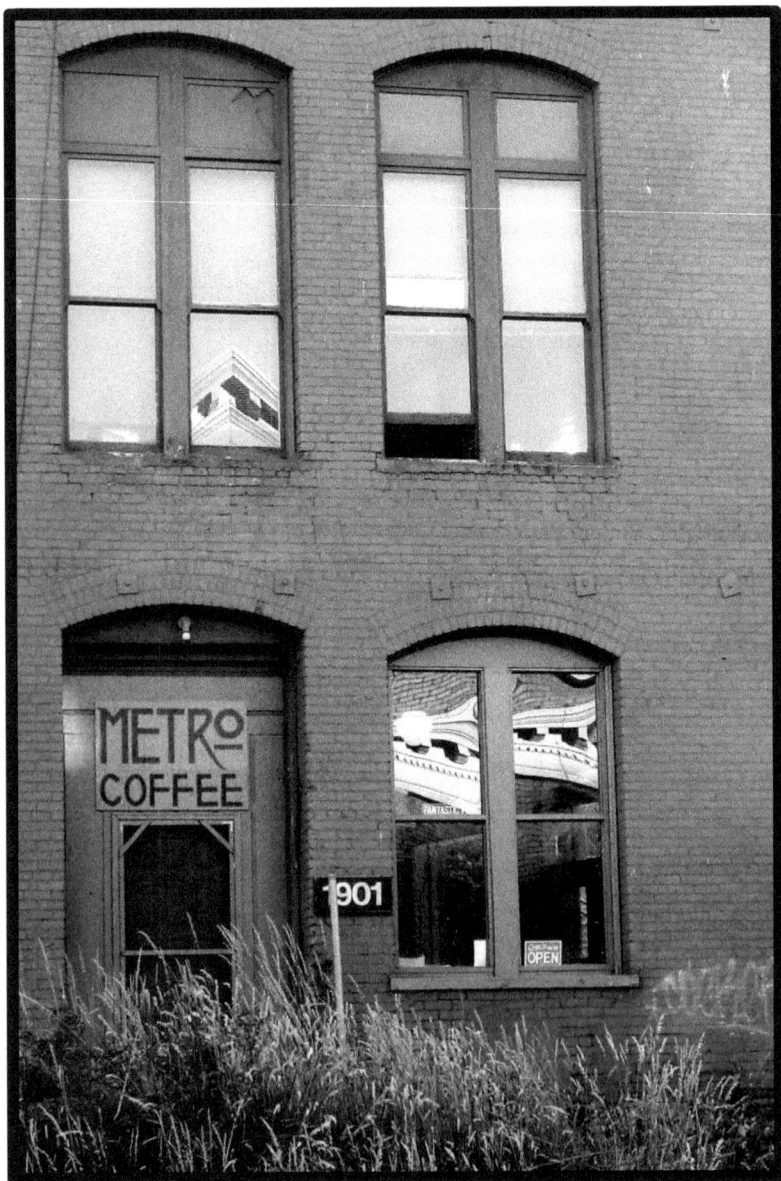

A Morning Cup of Coffee

Chilly spring morning
Nice solid smallish white coffee cup
Like in the '50s

No pretension
No post-tension
No ascension

Coffee's hot
A bit bitter
Just right

A poem is just a cup of coffee
On a cold spring day
Waiting for tomorrow

Reflections of
Restructured Realities

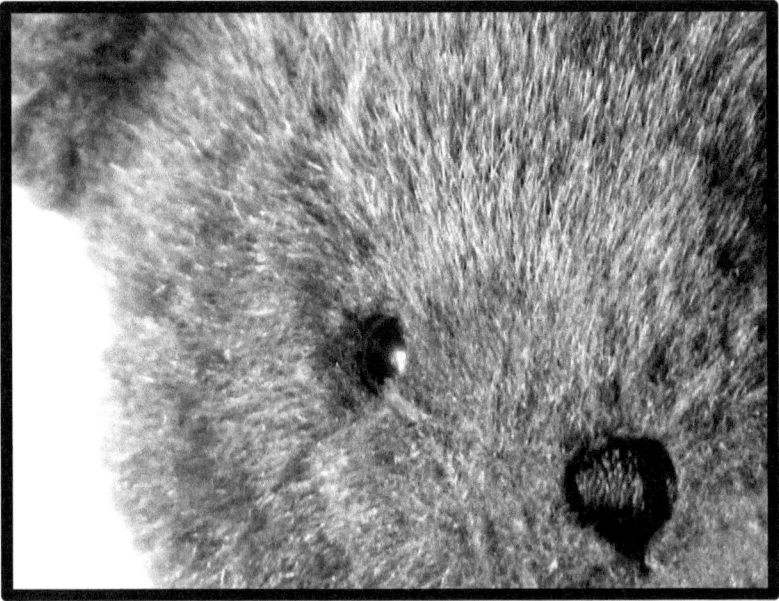

Grandpa Bought a Kite

The air smelled like apples
On a blue-sky day
With black birds
Flying high in the warm air

I was only three but I could talk
And of course walk
And feel the wind
On my soft face

And see my silly sisters and grandpa
Playing with something so red
That it hurt my eyes in the hot sun
And I thought it might be another bird

And it was another bird
And it flew flew flew away
Far far into the air
And it was red with the black birds

And I laughed at the bright red bird
And I tried to hug the blue sky
And I loved my sisters
And grandpa held my hand

Shadows

The brightest days
Cast the longest shadows
Stretching beyond telling
In the heat

A Kansas sunflower
Stretches to the horizon
In hot waves of
Shadowy illusions

Shimmering like a ghost
Of a heavenly star
Like a golden jewel
On the desolate Kansas prairie

The Conflicts and Marriage of Opposites

It is funny to consider
Sadness in the midst
Of smiles

For miles of littered
Emotional attachments
Unmentioned by the priests

Dressed in, of all colors,
Black to represent darkness
It seems to us night weepers

And daytime losers
Because even when the dice roll right
We lose, every time, in our minds

Capricious

Some days, I wish for a capricious God
Who might from time to time see me
As more than someone fabricated just to please Him
Even as the red red robin perishes outside my door

Even when bitterness wins
And goodness loses a battle or two
And holiness means a down-and-out fight
And honesty is hard

I would dance with such a God
I would clap my hands in joy
I would move my tired feet in celebration
I would say a blessed good-night in the soulful darkness

I Awoke

As the light began to rise
I rose too
With old companions

A bit of worry beginning
To find its morning place
In my mind

Anger angling for his spot
Of early awakening
Hoping to overshadow everything

Even hopelessness forged his position
Trying to grow with the day's light
As flowers in a garden

I shall quit watering them all some day
Until they shrivel and die
Leaving me at peace at last

Until that day fully blossoms
I shall leave them in bed, again, to rest
As I tread lightly through the morning

They are not bad companions
But troublesome if allowed
To stay too close for too long

Contrary

Beware of cathedrals
Beckoning as though
Truth resides in
Solidity

Truth does not align
With right angles and straight lines
But with the minds of men
And the hearts of flowers

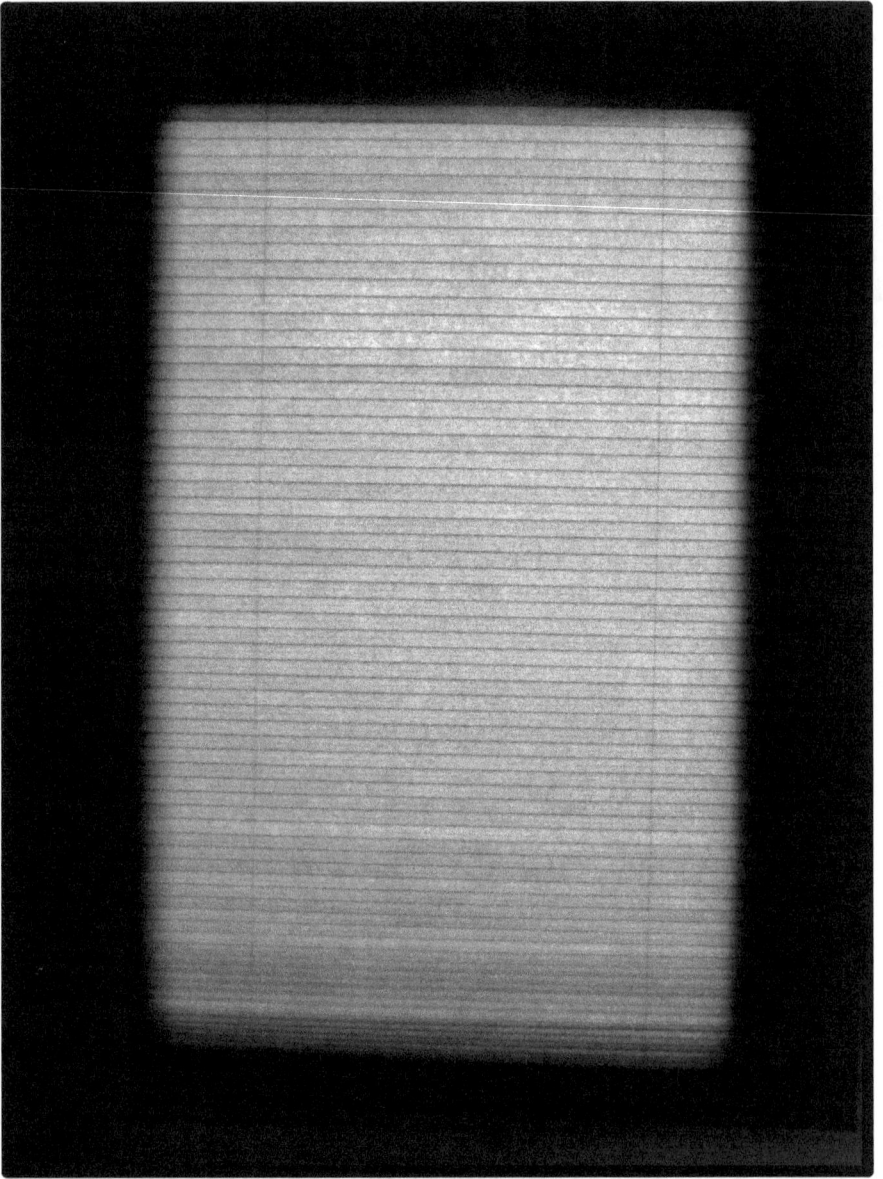

Apples and Gods

To some, apples and gods are a mystery
But living and dying
Prove gravity
To be the culprit pulling the holy fruit down

And gravity pulled me down one day
Into a darkened place
Where apples and gods
Were merely another weight

And apples and gods
And bounded hopes expired
And gravity
Just smiled

Wood

My cousin tells me that my father was a master in
Making things with wood, that his father and mine
Built barracks on the West Coast
That my father "carried" his father during those days

Would that my father had been a master in building himself
Finding a refuge in a world gone wrong
Building a resting place in the ashes
Caressing a wisp of cotton clouds in the storm

Would that my father had been a master in building himself
Would that his days had been less bruised
Would that his nights had been tender
Would that his sight had been clear

For we are here for barely a whisper
Within the flashing of the stars
And we are so fragile
Amongst the hardness of the world

The Beggar

In the soft silent snow
A ragged man and his dog
Sit like holy statues

Begging for a buck or two
Shivering on rough streets
In rough times

The man in the snow repeats his mantra:
"God bless you"
As I give him his hard-earned money

A cold man sitting day after day
With a good dog
Summoning kindness from a world gone wrong

Fear

Two plates for the morning meal
Again, after all these years,
As fear sat down with a weary sigh
With appetite diminished

We joined together to mark the day
He, old and frail,
His fierceness gone
His battles done

When light entered the room
He awoke with a familiar frown
And asked to be excused
And retired to bed, with covers

I, old also, my battles nearly done too,
Washed the plates and cups and forks and spoons
And put them away
And thought of fear, my old friend, again

We have made peace with one another
We both have our good and bad days
I will check on him soon
And tuck him in if he is cold

When I lie down for my final sleep
If a friend tucks me in
On that cold cold night
I will be satisfied

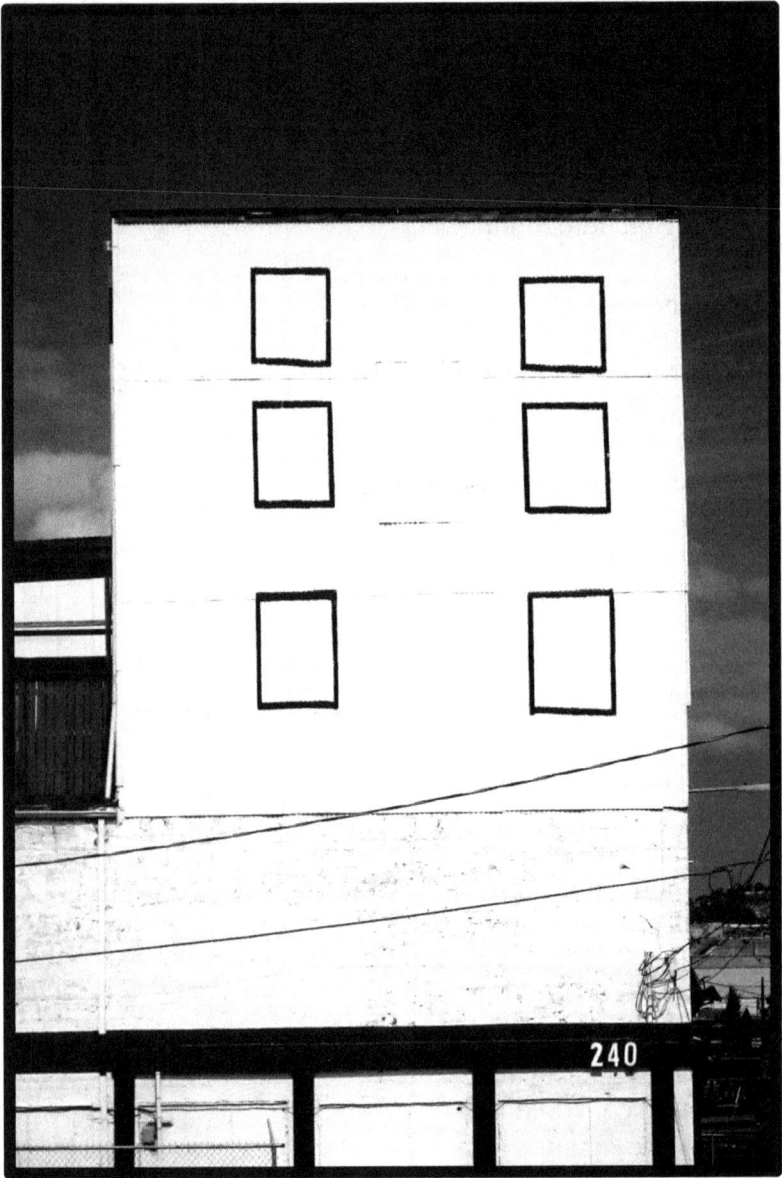

Existentialist Cheeseburgers

Hidden just beyond shadows
Lie round and square and diamond
Moments that can drive a mad man
Nearly to the brink of sanity

There is more truth in a good burger
In Las Vegas
Than all the red roses
In heaven

A sip of coffee
Drowns the blues
Every fucking day
Against long odds

Washing the Dishes This Morning

Washing the dishes this morning
I placed the saucers in the dish drying rack
(Or whatever they call the goddamn thing)

After putting two saucers in things did not look right
The saucers looked out of kilter
They looked dead wrong

I couldn't remember for sure though so I turned
Them around and felt their pure and celestial
Rightness immediately, viscerally

And then I thought no wonder
The world is so fucked up
We can't even remember how to correctly

And properly put the goddamn saucers into the
Fucking dish drying rack
(Or whatever they call the goddamn thing)

No Shame

There is no shame in sadness
No shame in fear
There is no shame in missing the party
When death is so near

The Bones of Our Children

In two thousand years
They will wonder about our forks
And spoons and knives
And plates too

They will debate our shoes
And our neckties
With scholarly attention
To metaphysical possibilities

Our toilets will mesmerize them into a frenzy
Of anthropological speculation as will our toasters
And television sets and our
Crumbled buildings and primitive sport arenas

They will have heard of our cold ways
Of starving the hungry and killing the dead
And they will ask themselves
"What drove them so crazy?"

Will they find answers in our treasures turned into garbage?
Will they discover our profound emptiness
In broken salt and pepper shakers
Or in the bones of our children?

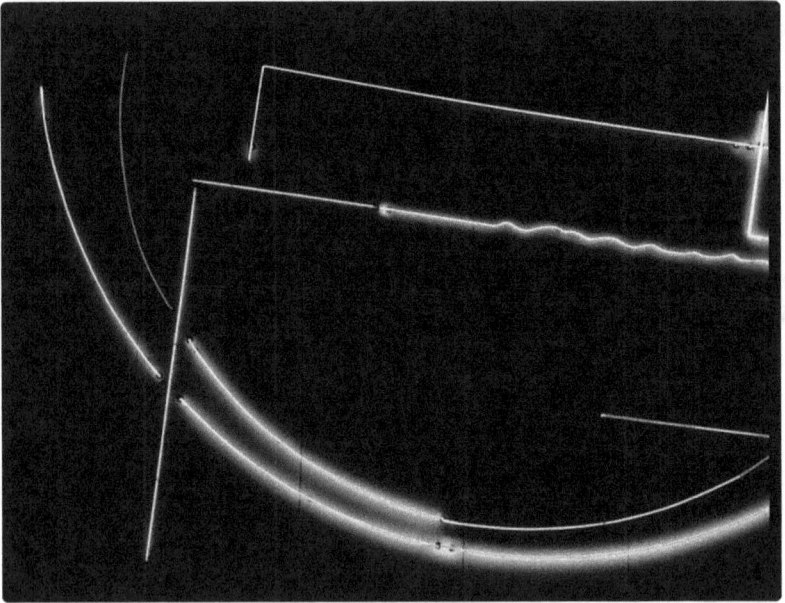

The Grim Reaper

Ah, there is no grim reaper
Grimly going about his deadly business

Nor is there a happy reaper
Joyously slaughtering

There is but the Grand Reaper Himself,
A waning moon in the darkening sky

Crazy, Baby

I am crazy and refuse sanity
As a child runs from a wild dog
Chasing him in the heat of the day

I shall never be someone else
Someone who properly counts
The concentric circles of metaphysical bullshit

As a way to hypnotize my mind
Into fitting in like a glove on a broken hand
Or like a white pressed shirt three sizes too small

Instead I will read a slow long book
Before I go to sleep and dream of moonbeams
Healing lost sheep in the night

Falling Gods and Sparrows Too

Does it really matter
Whether God

Sees the fallen Sparrow
Or the Sparrow sees God

Whether you speed through your life
Or idle your days and nights away

(Because upside down
Just might be right side up in the end)

Does God count the fallen Sparrows one by one
Do the Sparrows count the fallen Gods by the thousands

Holding On

I'm keeping it straight
So I don't bend
To the reality
Of being hidden
Within the dying breath
Of a cold winter

Hiding in the cellar
With my roots disguised so well
And hidden so deep
That I trust I will never stumble upon the steps
That could rip me from shadows
Tended for a lifetime

My Brother

My brother's mind
Is free-flowing
In a funky home
For free-flowing minds

In the blink of an eye
He flips from California
To the Kansas plains
And to the misty hills of Virginia

First he's home
And then he's gone
On the road
To oblivion

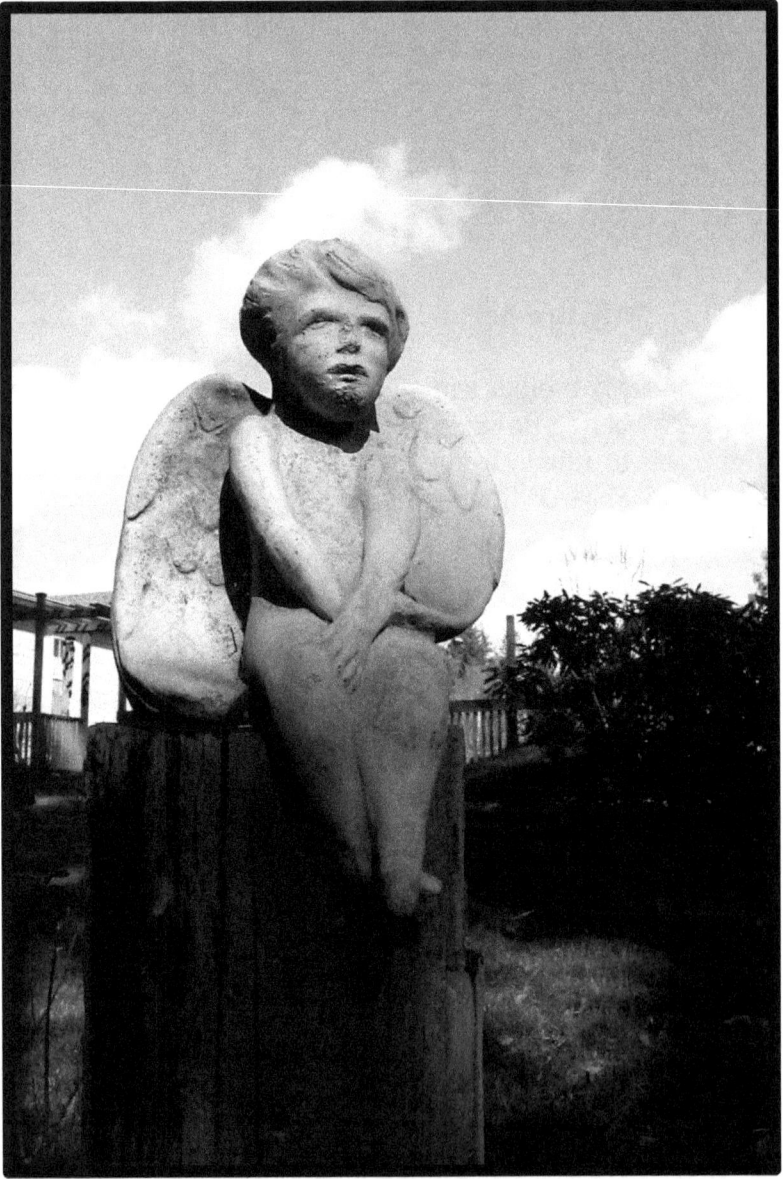

Hard Words

Sunshine does not settle sadness
Nor do soft words, whispered in soft darkness

The black crow cawing his desperation
Cannot be sanctified with a smile

The sweet song of the red robin
Is no finer than the cries of a child

The suffering of the hunted is surely as
Noble as the hunter

I pray that even God
Bows to a broken heart

Wired

I do not claim to fathom
The circling of the stars
Nor the passing of seasons
Nor of a heart's love

I do not claim to know
The arc of cause and effect
Traveling here and there
Unbound by earthly restraints

I sometimes believe
That magic wires dangle from the sky
And we are wired to invisible fate
In measures of a dream

Goodbye Mother, Goodbye Father

In a photograph
I see my father
And my mother
Before she died
When I was two

My father wears a fine hat
And a smart bow tie
Looking at the world
With eyes glaring like spotlights
As though it threatened him somehow

My mother is young and lovely
With her head gently
Touching my father
In love for the first time
Believing in joy

In time children are born
And losses come as they must
And love becomes so faint
That Mother and Father
Can no longer detect its dying glow

In a later photograph
My father and mother
Stand like strangers
On a frozen day
Barely touching

(Continued on next page)

My balding father stern and resigned
Wearing a dark suit and proper necktie
My mother nearly worn out it seems
With lost love and dreams

Ah, the world is filled with tragedy
And death will always win
With mothers and fathers and children
Blowing in the wind

Love

No Date

We never called it a date
Just a chance
To socialize
Meet someone new
Not a date

All day walking talking
Drinking too much coffee
Going to a movie, half way through
Whispering to each other
"It must be a comedy or something"

Standing together in an old house at two in the morning
After a simple good-bye hug
I walked to the door but turned around,
Going to her and kissing her softly on the cheek
It was so quiet, so still

Not a date at all

Change of Heart

She was not always easy to love
Angry and sullen at times
Slamming doors
Throwing telephones

At the age of nine, a fierce protector of righteousness
And protector of her mother
And I, childless by choice,
Would be a crappy fake father anyway

She said, "I will not go to the wedding"
To, "OK I'll go"
To, "OK I'll go, but I won't wear a dress"
To, "OK I'll wear a dress, but I won't be happy"

Years later, when she gave me a card one special day
That said, "Never forget that you are my Real Dad"
I glowed and glowed and glowed
With a heart that she had changed forever

143

144

Reunion

I did not know she was alive
I actually did not know that she was ever alive
I did not know that I had an aunt like her
My mother having died when I was two

She lived as a hermit in a small plain house
Outside a small town in Missouri
Where my mother came from
Both from the same dirt-poor poverty

I had no expectations for this reunion
With my mother's family
No memories
No hopes

She came out of the house alone
An old woman with wispy white hair
She said, "I remember you, Dale.
I used to hug you."

And with a gentle smile
She quietly opened her arms to me
And I sank into my mother's sister's arms
And I could hear myself breathing

And I could hear her breathing
And I could hear the Missouri wind
Kissing the Great Elm trees
In the barren yard

(Continued on next page)

145

My aunt looked like an angel to me
Pale and old and soft in her worn-thin, unpressed dress
Which flowed upon her
Like beautiful and soft pure white flowers

My mother, gone for 50 years
My aunt, from beyond my knowing
Beyond my understanding
Shimmering in the Missouri heat

* 9 7 8 0 6 9 2 6 2 5 6 0 6 *